LEARN CRICKET

With

VIV RICHARDS

LEARN CRICKET

With

VIV RICHARDS

A Young Player's Guide

Viv Richards

with David Foot

Stanley Paul

London Melbourne Auckland Johannesburg

Stanley Paul & Co. Ltd

An imprint of Century Hutchinson Ltd

Brookmount House, 62–65 Chandos Place, Covent Garden,
London WC2N 4NW

Century Hutchinson Australia (Pty) Ltd
PO Box 496, 16–22 Church Street, Hawthorn, Melbourne, Victoria 3122

Century Hutchinson New Zealand Limited
32–34 View Road, PO Box 40-086, Glenfield, Auckland 10

Century Hutchinson South Africa (Pty) Limited
PO Box 337, Bergvlei 2012, South Africa

First published 1985
© Viv Richards 1985
Reprinted 1986
All rights reserved

Set in Plantin Light

Printed and bound in Great Britain by
Butler & Tanner Ltd, Frome and London

ISBN 0 09 159841 9

CONTENTS

ACKNOWLEDGEMENTS

We are grateful for the cooperation of Somerset County Cricket Club; of the Headmaster, the Master in charge of Cricket, Roger Smith, and the boys of Taunton School. Our special thanks go to Derek Evans, responsible for many of the excellent technical photographs, and to Patrick Eagar and Adrian Murrell for other illustrations.

When it is accepted by common consent that I. V. A. Richards is as good, and arguably better, than any of his illustrious compatriots, it elevates him into a very high plane indeed. As his is a most individualized art, it is wrong to compare him with Headley, Worrell or a right-handed Sobers. Each is his own man and Richards is so lavishly talented that, like Compton, he is able to scorn the textbook. . . . His philosophy is a chilling message to the bowler and is simply that the ball is there to be hit. . . . Many must yearn for the day when English batsmen take a leaf from his book and put bat to ball. So many of our modern batsmen submissively allow the ball to come to the bat and are content to be dictated to by the most modest bowling.

Alec Bedser, Cricket Choice (1982)

I believe that Vivi's greatest contribution to his country was his affinity to, and rapport with, the youths of the nation – especially those from the area where he grew up. I consider his work with the young in his community as his finest contribution because unemployment was high and they identified Vivian with their hopes and aspirations. Therefore, his success, consciously and perhaps subconsciously, inspired in them a feeling that even though they might not be world-class cricketers, once they applied themselves, they too could succeed in their chosen field.

Lester B. Bird, when Deputy Prime Minister of Antigua

If Hammond was the master of off-side play, Richards and May may be described as supreme on the leg side. In addition, the way Richards can merely lean on the ball to send it scorching through the covers is only by perfect timing, positioning and balance. To me, Viv has it all. A little overconfident at times? Maybe, but he fits exactly my conception of the truly great batsman with the right approach . . . a little gamble with fate now and again, a little impatience to get on with it. If that be a fault, please give me more with similar defects.

Denis Compton, Compton on Cricketers (1980)

INTRODUCTION

I am setting out on this book with one unwavering intention – to convey my approach to the game of cricket. And if it has rather more to do with fun, enjoyment and using your *natural* skills than the content of many coaching manuals, I honestly see no reason for apologizing.

In this book I view my job as guiding and encouraging youngsters who want to play. Many of you won't be particularly gifted. You may not get into the 2nd XI at school. But I like to think you all have one priceless quality – enthusiasm.

I'm going to build on that. Just ask most county captains which they prefer – eleven enthusiasts in their side or a succession of self-centred individuals who play only for their own batting or bowling average?

If you are a very average but enthusiastic young player, I'm talking just as much to you as to the star of your club side. Maybe with my words of personal and informal advice I can make you a better cricketer. That'll be a lovely bonus.

Winning at cricket can at times be a serious business. I don't want to take away that healthy competitive streak. During the match, your aim must always be to come out on top. A so-called contest in which the result has no relevance is a pointless exercise.

But also play with a smile on your face. When I started out, back in Antigua, the cricket was full of chuckles. There were always good-natured remarks flying around. I can still see Tyrone 'Pacer' Williams knocking over all three stumps and then offering the ball to the batsman: 'Go and put that in the freezer, man!'

A happy approach on the field should never be interpreted as a lack of discipline. The two are completely different. But if your enjoyment of the game is evident, it is conveyed to the spectators. And the mood is determined for a good day's play.

The last thing I have set out to do in this book is to conflict with the coaches. They have their own ideas – and I agree with most of them. The standard of coaching, often in difficult circumstances and in the face of inadequate facilities, can be splendid.

My attitude to coaching was formulated by my own experiences as I grew up in St John's. We usually had to compromise, as boys, when it came to practice. The ground could be uneven, and that taught us the need to remain razor-sharp. We hurled stones to build muscles and improve our throwing arms. One trick, I remember, was to aim at the stems of hanging mangoes. Then, as the mangoes dropped, we'd sprint forward and catch them before they hit the ground or fell into the dirty water in the gutter. All good for fielding practice.

No formal coaching

I received little formal coaching and I don't think I've suffered because of it. I have watched my heroes and listened to my elders. The rest has been me.

So many mistakes have been made in the history of cricket. Well-meaning advisers used to shake their heads at the sight of a naturally gifted player who happened to be unorthodox. 'Don't do it that way, son. Look, this is how the coaching books say . . .' What a waste of talent! The intelligent thing to do is build on those natural skills. If a boy cricketer is discouraged from something he does so well, though in his own way, he'll get in a terrible mess and will end up tentative and half-hearted.

There are school players, of course, who are making such bad technical mistakes – maybe in the way they are hitting across the line – that they simply have to be put right. My ideal coach is the one who builds on natural strengths and, at the same time, sorts out technical tangles. The game is evolving all the time. Shots, stances and mannerisms that once were not acceptable aren't so likely to upset the purists these days.

I'm not in favour of too much theory. 'Do it this way – and you'll get this result,' the manuals say. But then I think of Colin Croft who supposedly did

it all wrong. He bowled very wide of the crease and still got the ball to leave the bat. I'm not sure that Colin knew how he managed it.

In a book called *Cricket Choice*, published in 1982, Alec Bedser said some very flattering things about me. Then he went on to say, 'Richards can do what other batsmen cannot do and he is not one for the young to try and copy. Some of his audacious shots would be suicidal for others and are not to be recommended.' He was probably thinking of my swing over extra cover after I've made space for myself. Elsewhere in this book I explain that this is a shot for limited-over cricket only. Yes, I do leave my stumps wide open and there is a big element of risk.

Mr Bedser may also be referring to the ball that I take from my off stump and put away through the on side. I could see people shaking their heads whenever I played it. 'That'll never do, Viv, you're defying the textbooks,' they told me. And when in England, where the wickets are slower and produce some movement for the bowlers, I was apt to get trapped L B W or pop up a catch to mid-wicket.

The fact is that I acquired the shot in the West Indies, where the wickets are hard and reliable. Despite a few dismissals – and those shaking heads – I've kept it in my English repertoire. Frankly, it's a shot that has brought me a lot of runs and gives me pleasure. It's one of my little specials.

Do your own thing

I want to encourage you to have your 'specials'. Never be afraid to do your own thing. If your individual approach ensures some success for yourself and your team, don't reject an allegedly reckless shot out of hand. When it becomes your regular downfall, however, then is the time to have another think.

There's an old saying: 'Different strokes for different blokes (or folks).' Concentrate on what you can do best. And remember at all times: the team is more important than the individual.

We've all had our models or heroes. In my case, it goes back to the wonderful Frank Worrell and Everton Weekes. Then came Clive Lloyd. I used to find myself copying the way he walked and the way he carried his bat. When I was a lad, seeing my first Test at Bridgetown, another hero of those days, Lawrence Rowe, even gave me his gloves as a keepsake.

Watch as many first-class matches as you can. Learn from that superb square cut of Gordon Greenidge. Admire the beautifully timed cover drive of Surrey's Trevor Jesty, who has always seemed to me to play it better than anyone else in England over recent years.

If you're a naturally attacking batsman, no doubt you like the style of Ian Botham. He's a power player. He doesn't caress the ball – he gives the impression that he has got something against it! And, above all, he's an entertaining player.

We all need a big slice of luck somewhere in our cricketing careers. I had mine when dear old 'Nookie', the umpire, didn't give me out the day Len Creed came to watch me in Antigua – and when Colin Cowdrey wrote a favourable paragraph about me in *The Cricketer* to start everything off – and when Brian Close came to take charge of Somerset – and when . . .

I'm also lucky to have the quickness of eye that allows me to pick up the ball very early, innate timing, strength and strong wrists. Sit down and work out your good points. Now start building on them.

They tell me I also give the bowler a chance. I'm not sure I want to agree with that. The point, I imagine, is that my style of play is not based on the occupation of the crease above all else. Yet I like to prove that I have an advantage over the bowler. That confidence must be evident.

If you are a schoolboy batsman, walk to the wicket in the next game as though you are on the way to a maiden century. You may only be pretending but don't let the bowler sense that. The moment you stumble out, giving the impression that you don't expect to last more than half a dozen balls, the fielding side will be rubbing their hands in glee. Never reveal an inferiority complex. As far as the bowler knows, you are the star batsman of your team.

And the same applies to the bowlers. Walk tall and look every inch a wicket-taker. Your job is to make the new batsman fear your ability, whether you are a lively seamer or an old-fashioned tweaker.

The psychological battle between batsman and bowler is one of the most fascinating aspects of cricket at any level. It's up to you to prove you're the boss. Sometimes in the county game, when I'm facing a slow bowler who I know isn't the best fielder to his own bowling, I deliberately crack back an apparently forward defensive stroke with more power than he expects. My intention is to make his hands burn. To imply that I don't think much of his bowling. To get him worrying. If you are a young batsman, learn to relish your battle of wits with the bowler. And vice versa.

Mental battles

I can't emphasize too much that you should always keep ticking away mentally. Cricket may seem pretty physical when the bowler starts on his fearsome run-up or the batsman puts a six into the cabbage patch. But it's a game of the mind. Even if you're a fielder who hasn't touched the ball for a dozen overs, still involve yourself mentally with every delivery.

Some of my most challenging mental battles have been with the leg spinners. There aren't so many of them about and so I look on them as special. There have been times when they have given me trouble. I can admire the gifted ability of someone like Pakistan's Iqbal Qasim. England has real problems at times against the spin in India.

Based on my varied experiences as a batsman around the world, I'd like to pass on one earnest piece of advice. When you stand, still and alert, waiting for the next delivery, don't bother your head in the least with the bowler's fancy run-up, the fact that he's six feet tall or that his arms are going round like a ferocious windmill. Concern yourself with one thing only – that little red cherry. Focus your eyes on the ball and never lose it.

Cricket is about runs and wickets. It is also about friendship. It's a point I don't want to ignore in a book like this, primarily written for young readers of vastly varying talents with long playing careers ahead of them. Some of my strongest and longest friendships were made through the game. When I go home to St John's, I still see the boys I once played cricket with at school, and the older men with whom I used to talk about Headley, Worrell, Weekes and Walcott.

When I came to England first I lodged at Bath. I made friends there, black and white, and I see them again every year when I play at the Bath Festival. I'm blessed with a good memory and I never forget a face. And, of course, I've got many wonderful friends within the game.

Just as cricketing friendships are important to me, so is my family. There's always the joy of getting home after one of my distant tours and discovering how much my children have grown up while I've been away.

This isn't one of those grim comprehensive instruction books, full of oppressive advice and technical knowhow.

It's a very personal account of how I play the game – and how I'd like you to play it, irrespective of the amount of talent you have.

Play it with a smile. Play it as nature intended you to. Play it with the mind as well as the muscle. Play it simply as well as you can. Play it positively.

And here's to a good season!

BATTING

THE CASE FOR COMFORT

Apart from a few kind words from old schoolmasters, my father, friends in Antigua and Alf Gover, I've had little formal coaching as a cricketer. Long ago someone said to me, 'Make sure you feel comfortable, Vivi.' I was never offered shrewder or better commonsense advice.

Cricket books have devoted miles of print to telling you how to stand at the wicket, for instance. I say, 'Stand in a way which is right for you.' That coincides so often, in any case, with the approved way.

Take those controversial backlifts of Tony Greig and Mike Brearley. They had the so-called experts shaking their heads. Now we hear that Archie MacLaren and Maurice Leyland were apt, at times, to do exactly the same. So what's new? There is certainly quite a large number of first-class cricketers who don't ground their bat as the bowler comes in. They feel it gives them an added chance of being ready against the quickies. Personally I like to 'tap away' on the ground as the bowler approaches. That is part of the necessary rhythm for me – it's rather like music.

As far as the stance is concerned, the important thing is to be perfectly balanced, to be able to move backwards or forwards with no difficulty at all. Keep the feet a few inches apart. I like my hands on the bat to be almost interlocking, but do what is right and natural for you.

Geoffrey Boycott used to practice in front of a mirror. It helped him stand in an ideal position and reassured him when it came to backlift. Many schoolboy players have resorted to the bedroom mirror – there's nothing conceited about that.

Young players worry unnecessarily. 'What weight of bat should I have, Viv?' Predictably my reply is, 'Whatever feels right for you.' I tend to vary.

On the slower tracks – in India and England – I'm inclined to have a heavier bat. In Australia or the West Indies, my bats are lighter. But don't get neurotic about it. When you find a bat that seems just the job, stick with it. Runs come just the same.

THE STANCE: People tell me how *still and relaxed* I am at the wicket. I think that is something you should aim at – it goes with the feeling of *comfort* I've emphasized. Note that the hands are close together, and the forward shoulder is pointing at the bowler. As for the feet, they are parallel with the line of the wicket. They are slightly apart, one on each side of the batting crease. And the weight is evenly distributed, so that it is equally easy to go backwards or forwards

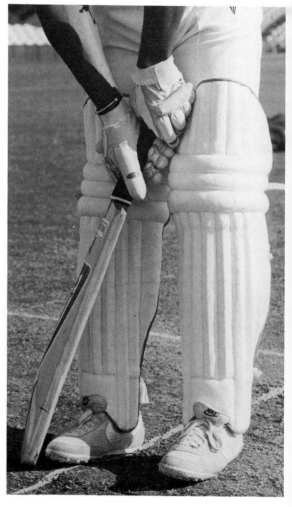

ON DEFENDING YOUR RIGHTS

Some young players have a strange idea that every ball is there to be hit. Maybe they watch too much one-day cricket on television.

It's crazy, as a batsman, not to acknowledge the virtues of the bowler. There are going to be some deliveries, of perfect line and length, that simply have to be treated with the greatest respect. That is when the batsman's job is to protect his wicket.

I'm not by nature a defensive batsman. But there are occasions when I get a great deal of pleasure from revising my approach and going into my shell. Not too often, mind you! There are times, though, when it is essential, in the interest of the team, to play the forward defensive stroke more often than usual.

When you reach the wicket it's advisable first to assess the bowling strength, to get a feel of the track and acclimatize yourself to the light and conditions. The forward defensive stroke provides a breathing space.

The front foot goes to a position alongside where the ball will land. The knee bends slightly and the heel of the back foot rises from the ground in a stretch movement. There must be no deviation in the straightness of the bat.

Take a look at the illustrations. Note the angle of the bat at the moment of impact, ensuring that there isn't the remotest chance of the ball spooning up into the air. Note the important role all the way through of the thrusting elbow.

If you're right-handed, the right hand plays a subordinate part in the stroke. It depends so much more on the left arm and hand. That's why coaches so often teach schoolboys to play the forward defensive stroke with one hand.

Above all, *make sure that there's no daylight between bat and pad*. There's nothing worse for a batsman than being bowled 'through the gate'.

At times, according to the pitch of the ball, you'll need to play the backward defensive stroke. As you move back, you'll remain side-on, in effect, looking over your shoulder. Go up on your toes and calmly let the ball come onto the bat.

FORWARD DEFENSIVE: Here are two different angles of the stroke, following of course the straight backlift that precedes it. These are a few points on which to concentrate: have the head directly over the ball at the moment of impact . . . leave no gap between bat and pad . . . notice the way I bend the forward knee and the position of my shoulder . . . move the full face of the bat along the line of the ball . . . get the angle of the bat right . . . now let the ball come to you, don't go anxiously in search of it

BACKWARD DEFENSIVE: You are using the area between the batting crease and the stumps. So when you come back don't be half-hearted, but step vigilantly onto the line of the approaching ball. Your weight is going to be transferred to the back foot but you must also leave yourself a forward poise. Get the head right over the ball – and don't you dare take your eyes off it. Otherwise, you can end up popping a simple catch to a close-in fielder. Note that left shoulder and high elbow

Give the ball the full face of the bat. The bat and elbow should end up in almost a vertical line

Opposite, top:

FORWARD DEFENSIVE: 'Grip that bat as if you're very much in charge', I tell my young pupils. Don't have the hands too far apart. You can run into problems if the right hand drops too low on the handle

Opposite, bottom:

The left hand is the one in control. So practise with one hand, acquiring the rhythm and feel of the stroke

NOT BRUTE FORCE

There's a tendency for young cricketers to believe the only way they are going to score boundaries is by brute force. Come off it! No one loves hitting fours more than I do – but I rely on coordination and timing.

The off drive is a lovely and popular shot. It's the one the spectators applaud most of all. That is because it has so much style and grace. I used to watch great players back in the West Indies stroking the ball through the covers and when I set out as a cricketer myself I was very much an off-side player, something which may surprise quite a lot of you.

OFF-DRIVE: A generous backlift. Then point your head and left shoulder in the intended direction of the stroke. Your weight goes on to your left foot. Ensure a clean follow-through. And don't let the head go aimlessly into the air

The ball has to be well pitched up for the off drive. And that is the cue for your left shoulder (I'm assuming you are a right-hander – reverse the process if you aren't) to spring into action. The shoulder thrusts forward, positively.

Forgive the refrain, but again it's absolutely necessary to get to the pitch of the ball. This is the basic secret with every assertive shot. If you only get halfway there you are heading for disaster.

The head must be quite still. The eyes must never deviate – they watch that ball like a hawk. The mind is made up. The weight is switched to the front foot.

At this point the job is only half done. The rhythm has to be sustained. The follow-through is a vital contribution. I promise you, the end result will be a winner in every sense. There's nothing sweeter in cricket than the moment of perfect timing when you intuitively know your shot is destined for the extra cover boundary.

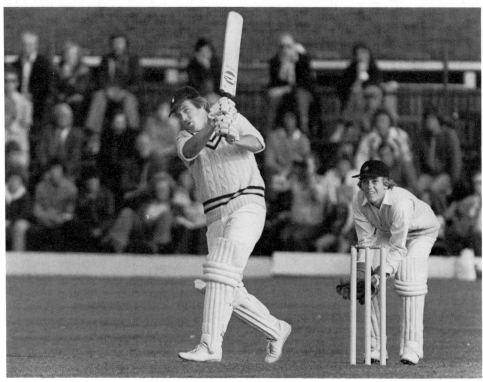

THE CHECKED DRIVE: It's important to know when you have to pull back – a mixture of intuition and discipline. Notice that I've kept the bat face open and on the line of the stroke. My upper elbow is high and the shot has been checked with my top forearm and bat in an almost perfect line

Opposite:

Above: I can't improve on Trevor Jesty when it comes to the cover-drive. The balance is perfect – and so is the timing. *Below:* His leg-side shots are equally assured

CUTTING THINGS FINE

'Hey, Viv,' young cricketers are always asking me, 'how do I play the square cut?' I never have any problem giving advice on that one. 'Just watch Gordon Greenidge,' I tell them.

Gordon is probably the best in the world when it comes to the square cut. He plays it beautifully and his timing can never be faulted. And you'd be surprised how many runs he compiles that way.

It's a lovely shot but it's also fraught with dangers. Too many adventurous young players choose the wrong ball – one that perhaps isn't wide enough of the off stump – mistime the moment they have to come down on the delivery . . . and give a simple catch.

Unless you're a master of the square or late cut, you are playing a dangerous game. Maybe the slip area is full of fielders. When you cut the ball, you are throwing out a bold challenge to them. You are rather arrogantly

---

SQUARE-CUTTING: It's a matter of fine judgment – and timing. You are coming down on the ball from above and there isn't much room for error. Don't start taking liberties with off-spinners and in-swing bowlers, or the balls that are lifting dangerously. Turn your head and shoulders into the line of the ball and put your weight onto the right foot. You meet the ball with the full stretch of the arms. The wrists have an important role to play and there needs to

saying, 'My timing is too good for you and, in any case, I can keep the ball down.' Well, all I'm going to say is 'Good luck!'

With the square cut, *select the right ball*. All sorts of things have to be considered, not just the distance of the delivery from the stumps. The natural bounce of the track is a factor. Don't start getting over-ambitious when you know realistically you can't rely on an even bounce, particularly when you are facing your early overs.

The transfer of weight to the back foot is a matter of controlled rhythm. The toes point at right angles to the wicket. And you must be absolutely spot on when the bat comes down firmly on the ball.

Playing the late cut is equally full of risks, especially when you are facing a cunning slow bowler and both short gully and slip are waiting to pounce. In this case, you move your back foot firmly across the stumps, with your toes this time towards third man.

Again, the moment of impact must be decisive and downward. There's nothing more disastrous than a tentative cut.

---

be controlled power in the stroke. The square-cut can be a valuable and attractive addition to the attacking repertoire . . . provided you're selective! It's normally played off the back foot, of course. Played off the front foot, to a really short and wide ball, the batsman is committing himself earlier. When the left foot goes forward, it mustn't be too far to the off – there must be enough room left to play the ball with a horizontal bat

The square-cut *par excellence*, as demonstrated by my Test colleague Gordon Greenidge

Watch Gordon Greenidge and some of the other masters of the cut. I've always been very envious of the superb way he plays it. To me, the late cut can be very delicate, very rewarding – and very, very dangerous if you haven't yet acquired the special knack.

A final word about the late cut. It's often fine against the leg-break or left-arm bowler when the ball is continuing to move away. But don't have too many fancy ideas of trying it out against the off-spinner!

EXTENDING THE REPERTOIRE

It has often seemed to me that many school coaches are inclined to concentrate on the cover drive and rather ignore the on drive, because it supposedly doesn't look so good and isn't so fashionable.

After coming over to England I consciously worked on extending my range of shots. That meant learning to pick up more runs on the leg side. Believe me, they are there for the taking. And I'm not advocating a wild orgy of pulling and cross-batted vigour.

Let's take the neat, controlled on drive, aiming for the area just wide of mid-on's right hand. Much of my advice in the case of the off drive again applies. The left hand is providing much of the control, the right hand the added power (once more I'm talking to right-handers).

Don't become sloppy and ungainly. The on drive can look very good indeed. But hold back on the temptation to belt the ball a little too hard. How often do we see players, having decided it's a delivery worth hitting on the leg side, playing across the line.

Use the full face of the bat. As you start your follow-up, it should be possible to draw a straight line from the left shoulder down the left arm and along the bat.

The on-drive can, in the early days, prove difficult. It'll repay additional practice. Once again, look at the illustrations and the important emphasis on balance, calm control and redistribution of weight onto the front foot.

I've already had a word or two about those rather more unorthodox clips of mine through mid-wicket off the ball pitched on the off stump. Sorry, lads, I'm not bringing it too much into this section. But by now you'll know my views on a few shots that you won't find too readily in the coaching manuals.

THE CLIP: Yes, this is my so-called special and I had to be talked into including this little sequence of my favourite 'clip' through the mid-wicket area. No, it isn't necessarily one for the strictest purists but it comes naturally to me and I don't really believe in rejecting something that brings you runs just because it's not found in all the best books. I'm talking of the ball that comes on the middle or off stump (some of my friends claim OUTSIDE the off stump!) which I whip through mid-wicket. Remember that I've been decisive and got to the pitch of the ball in the first place. My feet aren't too far apart. It can be quite profitable to me when I'm facing, for instance, an in-swing bowler whose delivery is naturally straying to leg. In honesty I have to advise you not to try it unless you feel very much in control – and are fully conscious of the pitfalls. And I suspect some of your coaches would prefer you to forget all about it

Opposite:

THE ON-DRIVE: Played correctly, this one can be every bit as good-looking and rewarding as the more popular off-drive. Most batsmen pick up a high proportion of their runs from drives in front of the wicket. Here, Clive Lloyd shows how. Start with a high back lift; this will provide you with the necessary power and the fluency for the shot. Timing is, of course, one of the basic keys. You work out the line of the ball and move forward more or less the same as for the forward defensive shot. But this time you hit the ball near the front foot and keep going along the direction of the stroke. Your follow-through will be towards mid-on

THE PULL SHOT: It's a rich source of runs, though some would say not the most handsome to look at. Runs, provided they are acquired intelligently while avoiding the more obvious mistakes, are ultimately of more importance than mere appearance. What's the good of the batsman with all the perfect postures if he can't make runs. The Pull is played successfully against the short-pitched ball from the medium-paced or slow bowler, the full toss and the long hop. For the full toss, ease the front foot towards the ball and hit it with your arms at full stretch with a downward cross-bat action. Try to pull forward of the square-leg umpire. For the long hop, you should move your back foot across to ensure your head is behind the ball. Keep your feet well apart so there is no loss of balance at the vital moment. The Pull also needs a good follow-through in the direction of the shot

HOOKERS LIVE DANGEROUSLY

More arguments probably rage over the hook than over any other shot in the game. And no doubt a kindly coach or father has told you at some time or other, 'Don't bother with it.'

You will have gathered that I don't exactly go along with this philosophy. *Cricket without a sense of adventure is nothing.* There's a big difference between the occasional calculated risk and a hellbent and ridiculous disregard for the rules of the game.

Somerset used to have a wonderful batsman called Harold Gimblett, an attacking opening batsman good enough to play for his country. And the first time he played at Lord's, in front of a few prewar old fogeys, this novice cricketer horrified the MCC members by hooking sixes.

There were all sorts of tut-tuts. 'Cut it out. It isn't an *approved* shot,' he was told. Wisely he ignored his detractors, improved his hooking technique and found the shot a rich source of runs.

Ian Botham is something of an expert – from both points of view. As a bowler he deliberately encourages unwary batsmen to hook his short-pitched deliveries. And as a batsman he's renowned, of course, for his sixes over square leg and long leg.

My own advice is that if you've got an aptitude for the shot and obey a number of basic rules then there's nothing wrong with trying your luck.

First, a word of common sense. Be very conscious of field placings. If the bowler has a couple of deep fielders strategically placed for a miscalculated hook shot, then make doubly sure that you don't fall for it. So many players in the county game as well as lower down the scale make a hash of the hook. The result is a simple catch – and anger all over the batsman's face.

It's essential, when playing the hook, that you *get into position very quickly*. That can still mean leaving your options open. It may be that the ball, having been dug in short, just doesn't come up, inviting itself to be hooked. Or it may rear up too high altogether. In that case, let it go harmlessly over your shoulder.

Here's something to remember. Short-pitched deliveries aren't always deliberately schemed. They can be downright bad balls – and deserve to be punished. I'm not the sort of bloke who likes to let a bowler get away with a loose, inaccurate delivery. Let him have it!

But try to *keep on top of the ball*. Having moved the back foot back across the body and having determined that everything is right for the hook, roll your right wrist over the left (in the case of the right-hander) to ensure that the ball doesn't go high into the air.

Some young players are reluctant to play the hook shot because they think they are exposed to being hit. There's a measure of self-preservation in all of us. But try not to be afraid. Fear can be very counterproductive when it comes to batting.

Provided you haven't wasted any time getting into position and you keep your eye intently on the ball, you should go home in one piece.

THE HOOK: This is for the short-pitched ball coming up at waist height or probably higher. Your balance is going to be put to the test here. You shift your right foot and body back and far enough to the off to be outside the line of the flight – and then you hit the ball over your left shoulder. But you need to get into position quickly. Wrist control, with the right wrist rolling over the left one, minimises any chance of a catch. It's a brave shot and, as the ball is no doubt a straight one, you could be in all sorts of trouble if you miscalculate. Don't be impatient and try to start hooking too early in your innings – and be cautious when the bowler is getting movement from the leg. The whole body pivots in the process of the hook shot

Ian Botham demonstrates his exciting and extravagant hook

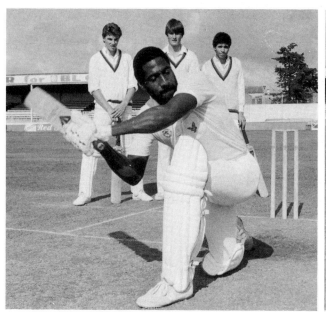

THE SWEEP: Yes, it's just as it sounds, the perfect description of the batsman's action. Again it's a rather specialized stroke that you should avoid unless you feel absolutely confident about it. It's played to the well-pitched delivery just outside the leg stump. As such it is a useful run-getter against the off-spinner or with the ball running away in that direction. And if the ball is straight and you miss . . . well then, there could be problems ahead. So cut out the risks. Get your left foot inside the line of the ball – that will help you to protect your wicket in the process. The Sweep isn't the most handsome stroke in the book but it justifies some practice, I promise you

Opposite:

THE STRAIGHT DRIVE: Most cricketers agree that this can be one of the most satisfying shots in the game. It's elegant and uncomplicated. You use a straight bat to stroke that ball back past the bowler. But make sure your left foot (right in Clive Lloyd's case) gets to the pitch of the ball. Don't be sparing with the backlift. The left arm (for the right hander) is the one fully in control. The bat is brought down absolutely straight and you hit through the ball in a rhythmic motion

GOING FOR THE BIG ONE

We all love a slogger. Every village team has one. He usually does it with a cross-bat and with his head in the air. He's good for entertainment – and often bad for bowlers' averages.

But if you want to become a first-class cricketer, do be realistic. You can't hit a six nearly every ball. You have to learn to play the bowling on its merit.

I've been as guilty as everyone else. I can think of many innings of mine that were brought to a premature end because I had a rush of blood to the head. But I relish going for the Big One.

Some batsmen don't really approve of lofting the ball. They believe it's their brief to keep everything on the carpet. That's all very well, but provided you try to hit straight and intelligently there is nothing wrong with lofted drives.

In fact, in one-day games sixes frequently become a necessity. My seemingly much discussed whack over extra cover from the ball on my leg stump is part of that scene. I'm apt to find myself confronted with a packed

leg-side field. So I occasionally take my life in my hands, step away to leg and aim to put the ball into the crowd over extra cover.

It isn't something I suggest you try. As someone who admires stylish and correct batting, preferably if it's entertaining as well, I privately reprimand myself for one or two of my more ambitious shots. You won't find them in the manuals. They have been paraded out of sheer necessity – and, I suppose, a sense of challenge.

It isn't clever to leave all three stumps exposed, ready to be knocked over. But, as I've already said, we have to be bold improvisers nowadays. If it's in your nature to chance your arm on the odd occasion, I'm not going to lecture you, but I will say this. Don't take a risk when the team can ill afford it. And don't make up your mind too far in advance. Those batsmen who predetermine their shots are asking for trouble.

Be discriminate, if you can. When the time comes – and the ball comes – for your mighty swish, remember that *timing is so much more important than sheer muscle*. Get to the pitch, remain utterly controlled, never for a second take your eye off the ball, hit straight . . . and may it be a six for you to cherish.

Whatever you do, once you have committed yourself, hit the ball with all the confidence in the world. Don't suddenly lose faith and check yourself.

THE LOFTED DRIVE: I fancy that one of mine is heading for the spectators over extra cover, a favourite of mine! My general advice to you is to hit as straight as possible. There's nothing wrong with lofting the ball – at the right time. It disconcerts the fielders and makes them move back. The main difference between going for a four and a six is that, for the four, you play the ball alongside the front foot. For the six, you play it six to nine inches in front. Most of us enjoy 'hitting over the top'. But it must be done in the right way. At all costs, avoid putting your head in the air. Keep your eyes focused on 'that little red cherry' all the time. The Big One isn't the result of massive muscle. It's the culmination of timing, composure and coordination. There must be a full back lift, the head and shoulders must lead positively and then let's have a spectacular follow-through. And good luck with the sixes . . . At times you will want to move out of your ground to drive the slower balls. That is fine, provided you assess the flight first. Down you go: left, right, left. But remember the basic rules, with final weight onto the left leg and eyes on the ball

SURELY IT'S WORTH A GLANCE

All batsmen get bogged down at some stage. They find it difficult to penetrate the arc of fielders, and time is ticking by.

The leg glance is perhaps one of the less glamorous and profitable strokes, but it should never be underestimated. How often have we seen a delicate little deflection to the fine-leg boundary – to the frustration of the fielding side. It repays a bit of practice and is a very useful, if modest, addition to the batsman's repertoire.

The glance, as you will know, can be played off either the front or the back foot. In the case of the front foot, the batsman leans forward as if he were

THE LEG GLANCE: For you to play this one off the front foot, as Allan Lamb is doing so successfully, the ball needs to be pitched on or just outside the leg stump. Here's the chance for you to show those magic wrists! Place your forward foot inside the line of the delivery, turn the face of the bat delicately at the moment of impact . . . and you could be good for a fine-leg boundary or, if there's a fielder down there, at least a composed single.

going into a forward defensive shot. But this time he gets his front feet inside the line of the bat. Then with a little twist of the wrists – and a measure of luck, which we all need – the ball is trickling away well wide of the wicketkeeper's left hand. Keep the bat close to the body or you'll be in a spot of trouble.

As for the leg glance off the back foot, it isn't as easy as it looks. Balance can be a distinct problem. The back foot retreats rather as in the backward defensive shot. And all the time the head is rigidly over the ball.

Deflections like this complement the more assertive front-foot attacking shots. But put them all together and you have every chance of keeping your score – and the team's – going along nicely.

The glance off the back foot, as I demonstrate, is to a ball rather short of a length. Move back assuredly and deflect it just in front of the left knee. But watch the ball like a hawk. The runs come from the bowler's momentum. The leg glance is something that justifies great patience and practice. When playing back, let the ball come *very close* before you turn the bat face

QUICKIE QUESTIONS

Q. Hey, Viv, how do I bowl yorkers like Big Bird?

A. Unless you are as tall as Joel, you don't! He's the master. The yorker is a terrific ball and batsmen, unless they're very lucky, can't score off it. Often an unwary batsman, completely deceived, swings over the top of it, and gets his castle knocked down. If you are a bowler who can pull out a fast yorker at the right moment, good luck to you. My advice to the batsmen? If you've a very high backlift you may be in trouble. Your job is to come down on that ball as fast and as effectively as you can. 'Dig it out,' I tell young cricketing friends. 'Just think you're digging your garden!'

Q. Hey, Viv, am I unusual in being superstitious about the same, dirty old bat week after week?

A. That's your choice. If it's bringing you the runs, then don't change your luck. I know first-class players who are incredibly superstitious – and the colour of their bat gets darker and darker. Others are always smoothing it clean with a piece of sandpaper. Me? I've got a few superstitions, but not about bats. There was a time when I picked up the one nearest to me in the dressing room. Honestly.

'I think I'll pull out a couple of yorkers in the next over,' Joel Garner is probably saying. The camera catches us at a serious moment. Maybe we're planning a batsman's downfall. As I advise you recurrently in this book: keep ticking over mentally. It's a big part of the challenge – and the enjoyment

Q. Hey, Viv, when I take guard, should it be middle or middle and leg?

A. I don't like to give advice on this. Experiment, and choose what is right for you. Remember that most first-class players take middle and leg (or 'two legs' as they usually say). Some prefer the leg stump. A good many players ask the umpire to give them guard from where the bowler bowls. Others argue it's more logical to be given it from where they will face LBW appeals – from behind the wicket.

Q. Hey, Viv, is it a fact that you and Ian Botham try to outchallenge each other during the course of a match?

A. A lot of people seem to think so but it's a fallacy. They see us chatting away and grinning, and jump to conclusions.

Q. Are slow bowlers easier to score off?

A. Not necessarily. Quite often with fast bowlers the batsman can simply guide the ball to the boundary. All the pace comes from the momentum of the delivery. Some batsmen have naturally sharp reflexes and are better when facing the seam men. Others' strength is being able to use their feet to the spinners. If you've a weakness against one type of bowling, work incessantly on that in the nets. And remember, all bowlers are human. They all send down bad balls.

Q. Hey, Viv, I like bowling bouncers. Do you approve?

A. Well, for a start, I don't expect you are quite as fast as some of the West Indies boys. In most club cricket, bouncers are wasted. And it's criminal if they merely take the shine off the new ball. If you fancy yourself in letting one go occasionally – and I did say *occasionally* – it's a fair ploy in the right circumstances.

Q. I like playing the sweep, Viv. Any words of advice?

A. Yes, so do I. Make sure you get your front foot inside the line of the ball – your stumps get guarded that way – and don't aim for too much muscle as you sweep downwards. It's a shot that needs control and coordination.

Q. Hey, Viv, what was your most dramatic match?

A. It has to be the time I turned out against St Kitt's – and had three ducks in the same game. But I'd rather not go into that!

Q. What's the number one attribute of a fielder?

A. Enjoyment. If he's bored in the field, he's wasting a lot of time on a Saturday afternoon.

Q. Hey, Viv, when do I bowl *over* the wicket and when *round*?

A. It's usually a matter of common sense. The conditions come into it, the pitch itself or the wind. Leg-break bowlers are well advised to stick to over the wicket. It's different for off-spinners. They are apt to switch to round the wicket to have a go at a left-handed batsman. There are also times when the ball is actually turning too much on a crumbling wicket. He will be able to offset this by going *round*. It gives him more chance of earning an LBW decision.

Q. Hey, Viv, I know I really should know. But can you tell me the difference in the grip for the *in* and the *out* swinger?

A. Never be ashamed of a lack of knowledge. We're learning all the time. You'd be surprised how many top players aren't always absolutely sure how they produce a particular ball. The great Maurice Tate used to say he didn't know why one of his deliveries went one way and the next one the other! Very basically, this is the only difference. For the out-swinger, you point the seam towards the slips with your first and second finger on either side of the seam. For in-swing, you point the seam towards fine-leg.

Q. Hey, Viv, should a full-toss be belted?

A. That's the temptation. But I've seen so many guys come to grief with that one. It can be a very useful ball for the bowler to throw in. He's taking a gamble, of course, and he may be punished. From a seat on the boundary, the full toss looks a gift but hitting a high one can get you into terrible trouble. So at least try to be selective.

Q. What's the worst mistake I can make as a batsman?

A. Failing to get your left foot close enough to the pitch of the ball – and having your head in the air.

Q. And as a *cricketer*?

A. By thinking you're more important than the team.

BOWLING

I know what you're going to say. The art of bowling is all cut and dried when it comes to the West Indies, with their clutch of fast bowlers. Of course it's an advantage if you have a succession of great speed merchants.

In 1984 I felt rather sorry for Gloucestershire. It wasn't just that they finished on the bottom of the championship table. It was the fact that although an encouraging number of their batsmen topped 1000 runs, their bowlers too often failed to take the wickets to complement what had gone before. There must always be a balance of batsmen and bowlers in any team. The best stroke-makers in the world mean nothing if their bowlers are a soft touch.

I don't put myself up as an expert. But I've done a bit in my time with those little seamers and off breaks – and I've been an interested observer of the breed for years. Occasionally, back in the West Indies and maybe on a summer's evening in England, I pull in to watch a local match for half an hour. One thing I notice is that too many club cricketers try to bowl too fast. The result is that they completely lose their length and line.

Joel Garner, my Somerset and West Indies colleague, is generally accepted as the most difficult bowler in the world to score runs off. Just as well we're usually on the same side! Look at those upstretched fingers – the '12 o'clock' action I refer to in this section. His height is, of course, a wonderful asset to him, allowing him so much *bounce*. But he can do so much with the ball . . . quite apart from his famous yorker. And another point for aspiring bowlers to remember – he wastes very little

The cardinal rule for any emerging young bowler should be to *aim at the stumps*. *Bowl straight*. Direction simply can't be ignored. There's always time to work up the pace afterwards. How often in club matches, and in county matches too, I'm afraid, do we see the new ball wasted.

The new ball is a magnificent weapon. In its opening overs it's capable of movement and all sorts of speedy detours in expert hands. But if it's only going to be hurled in the approximate direction of the stumps, and dug in short to no purpose at all, the fielding side might as well have stuck with last week's battered ball.

I'm a great advocate of variety. Don't go mad, you budding bowlers. But bowl with your head. Accept that *every delivery is a battle of wits between you and the batsman*. Keep him guessing. If he's looking apprehensive and wary, it's one up to you.

This brings me to my old Somerset pal, Ian Botham. 'Both' is at times criticized for his bowling and the fact that it is punished. You won't hear me criticizing him. He's never remotely negative. He'll try almost anything to get a wicket. He'll take liberties. He'll throw in an off-spinner in the middle of his outswingers. And the batsman never knows what is coming next.

The one thing the batsman wants is a predictable bowler, someone who can be relied on to keep pegging away with six similar deliveries every over. There are some of those bowlers about. They bowl entirely with their arms and never with their heads. Batsmen love 'em.

If you are a bowler by inclination, practise continually. Don't be satisfied, even if the wickets are beginning to come. Perhaps you have a natural ability to swing the ball away. Well, now is the time to learn how to master inswing as well.

Malcolm Marshall is, I accept, a pretty fearsome sight for wary batsmen as he pounds in like this. He's probably the fastest in the world – and just note the determination in his eyes. He is hungry for success, as every bowler must be. His focus is those three stumps at the other end. Study the angle he has made with his forward shoulder and forearm, so that he can look straight down the pitch. Malcolm is a fine model for young fast bowlers. There's an overall rhythmic style and composure about his run-up, delivery and follow-through. He practised incessantly before he became an established Test and county cricketer. Nothing comes easily. Experiment until you've found the right run-up for YOU. There's a temptation to make it too long – and you end up by wearing yourself out before you even reach the point of delivery

Can there be another Malcolm Marshall on the way? Ambition is a vital part of the game. Here I take a close-up look at one fiery young pupil. I'm looking for smoothness of run-up, coordination of movement and the encouraging signs that my young bowler isn't going to have a no-ball problem because of where he places his feet

Opposite top:

THE LEG SPINNER: And surely Pakistan's Abdul Qadir is the modern master. The two illustrations show us the magic in his wrists – and a deadpan expression which reveals nothing of his innate cunning. He has outwitted many of the world's greatest and most experienced batsmen. This isn't the kind of book to examine the offshoots of leg-spin . . . of googlies, top spin and the 'flipper'. All I'll say about the googly – the one that goes the other way – is that it's a marvellous part of the armoury. But don't try to overdo it, especially when you're young. It can become rather too much of a habit, will confuse you and even lose you the rare and treasured art of turning the ball from leg. Not all slow bowlers are expert spinners, of course. Instead they become specialists of flight. If you fancy yourself as a budding leg-tweaker, you need strength in your fingers, flexibility in your wrists and, above all, loads of imagination. It's rather easier and probably more natural to be an off-spinner but stick at your 'leggers'. Batsmen just aren't used to playing them – that's particularly true of England – and so you should revel in being a 'tormentor'. With so much involved, you may at times have trouble with your length. Never panic about that but do attempt to keep the ball up to the bat

Whether spin or seam, I tell my young pupils, get the arm well up

Plenty of left-arm bowlers around these days, it seems . . . all hoping to be a Bishen Bedi or a Derek Underwood one day. And why not? The grip is similar to that of the off-spinner – in reverse order. All the great slow left-arm bowlers are renowned for their nagging accuracy. Let that be your aim

Opposite:

GETTING TO GRIPS. (1,2) The first two close-ups show the way I hold the ball for my off-spinners, with my first two fingers well spaced. It's the index finger that does the most work in a motion that old coaches liken very accurately to turning a door knob in a clockwise direction. The leg-break, as I've explained with the Abdul Qadir illustrations, is harder to control because of the wrist movement involved. The grip is roughly the same as for the off-break but the fingers are closer together. The spin, with the anti-clockwise direction, comes largely from the inside of the third finger

SWINGING THE BALL: (3,4) If you want to get real movement in this way, don't try to bowl too fast. Humid conditions will be a big plus for you – and so always is a new ball. Yet you'll achieve little without good arm and body action, and of course getting the grip right. Figure 3 is the *in-swinger*. The seam is pointing towards fine-leg. Try to land it, well up, just outside the off stump. Don't turn the wrist at all. When it comes to the away-swinger, point the seam at first slip. Note the way I use my thumb in both cases. And a final word about all that polishing that goes on. Polish one side of the ball only. The rough, unpolished half is positioned on the side you intend (or hope) to swing the ball. Science, they tell me, does the rest. . .

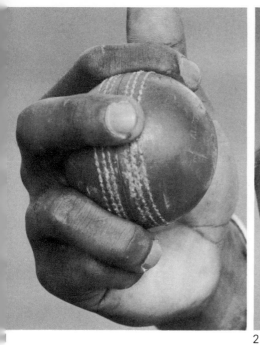

2

3

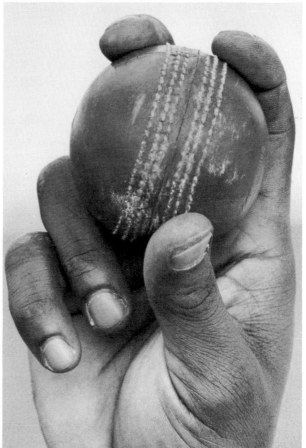

4

Aim for a smooth, rhythmic action. Bill Andrews, the former Somerset fast bowler and later coach, had a good action himself, one of the best of his day. He used to call it '12 o'clock high'. It's a graphic description, if you think about it. Learn when to come close to the stumps and when to go wide. Learn from others. Watch the first-class players. Television gives us all a marvellous close-up view.

West Indian bowlers are highly competitive. There's nothing wrong with that. We spend a lot of time over our team talks before a Test match. We plot how we shall deal with specific opposing batsmen, knowing their weaknesses.

However modest your standard, *study the batsman* you are facing. *Note his flaws.* If he can't use his feet and you are a slow bowler, then cash in.

Many batsmen are nervous at the start of their innings and, however much they try, they can't hide it. Spare them nothing. Put pressure on them straightaway. This is perfectly fair and valid. It has nothing to do with gamesmanship. You can still have a drink with them in the bar afterwards.

Some batsmen are notoriously suspect against pacy yorkers. That's the cue for your local version of Joel Garner to start pitching them right into the block-hole.

The conditions are invariably significant. On a humid day you may find the ball wobbling about all over the place. And perhaps you didn't think you could even swing the ball. Experiment, and adjust accordingly – and bask, by all means, in the compliments of colleagues and the confusion of the batsmen!

Don't be selfish and persuade your captain to overbowl you. Whether you concentrate on flight or finger spin, seam or swing (and a bit of disconcerting bounce), *never become a mechanical bowler.*

Sir Gary Sobers had a marvellous range of bowling styles, to suit all occasions. Somerset used to have a skipper, Jack Meyer, who liked to bowl six different balls in an over. Lancashire also had one called Cecil Parkin. Old Trafford dubbed him 'Bag of Tricks'. It may have been demanding for the wicketkeeper. But it was far worse for the batsman.

Temperament is important when it comes to the bowling. Slow bowlers may be incredibly accurate but they are going to be whacked at times. Batsmen will go down the wicket to them. And it may not seem like justice. The good spin bowler learns to wince and bear it uncomplainingly.

All slow bowlers get punished on occasions. If the experience is going to knock you off your length and destroy your morale, then my lighthearted advice is for you to switch to seamers.

FIELDING

Who wins matches for you? Is it the hard-hitting batsman – or the wily spin bowler? I become more and more convinced that fielders also, just as frequently, determine results.

It's an old saying, but you spend a lot of time in each game standing around in the field. If you don't enjoy fielding, you may as well pack cricket up altogether. Me? I honestly love every minute as a fielder. And it doesn't bother me too much where the captain puts me. Variety is part of the fun.

In my earlier days I was often at cover. Latterly I have found myself more in the slips. Persuade me in a confidential moment to reveal which position I like most of all and I'll tell you – in the outfield. That's why I often enjoy myself so much in one-day matches. Chasing around the boundary and then hurling the ball back gives me an incredible sense of boyish freedom.

Not everyone likes one-day cricket, with its frantic search for runs and surfeit of negative bowling. Yet one of its undeniable virtues has been the way it has improved the standard of fielding in England.

These are days of specialist fielders, whether in club or Test cricket. Maybe you are a natural slip fielder. Or one of those ever alert short legs, getting ready for the bat-and-pad chance or ducking in self-preservation. The beautiful cover point is one of the most stylish sights in the game. Specialize by all means. Indeed, I think that is wise. But also take the opportunity occasionally to field in a completely different role. It broadens your skills – and your understanding of the game.

The skills are so varied, of course. The outfielder becomes expert at judging the high, hanging catch, or when he can prevent the batsmen going for a third run. The close-in fielder has, by contrast, absolutely no time to think about it. He relies on reflex catches. They stick or they don't. A combination of intuition, anticipation and good luck ensures that more stick than slip away.

I mentioned the high catches just now. They always look so much easier from a boundary seat. Once you have assessed their range, get right under them and grasp the ball with both hands into the chest. Then immediately close the fingers. Avoid the embarrassment of moving into a perfect position and then letting the ball drop out of nervous fingers.

Graeme Fowler is caught in the fifth Test at The Oval. You can see the intense concentration on the face of both my captain, Clive Lloyd, and myself. The slip must remain ever-alert, on his toes, ready to pounce either to his left or his right

My young pupils from Taunton School join me in the slips. 'Feet apart, hands poised . . . and never a lapse in concentration,' I tell them

The ball is coming towards me on the boundary. The batsmen are contemplating just how many runs the shot is worth. But there must be no frenzied return from me. I mustn't snatch the ball. I want to 'feel' it firmly in my hand before returning accurately to the wicketkeeper. The whole process of the out fielder must be one of confident control. And, as I demonstrate, my eye must never stray for a fleeting second from the ball

In this case I've had to chase the ball, my back to the wicket. It means picking up one-handed. Again the overall action of the fielder must be controlled and sharp. Balance is important in the way I stretch down for the ball. As I turn I must be assessing the distance

You'll find most of the top-class cricketers often fielding the ball in this way. If the ball should bounce or deviate, my knee and body are behind as an additional barrier. It minimises the chance of a mistake

It's the high catch. Perhaps the ball seems to be hanging in the air – and the crowd is tense. I remain as still as possible, having made my ground. My hands are ready to grasp the ball as it drops, and to bring it safely to my chest. There must be no impatient snatch, no inclination towards anything spectacular. I haven't let the 'little red cherry' out of my gaze for a split second

Far more embarrassing, of course, is the spectacle of two fielders converging at great speed, colliding and missing the ball altogether. Let the whole ground (and the neighbouring parish) know your intention. If you think the catch is yours, shout at the top of your voice, 'Mine!' There can be no confusion then.

The number one rule for any fielder – whether gully or long on – is to *keep your eyes unwaveringly on the ball*. There must be no distraction and no indecision. That applies whatever the angle of the ball coming to you, or whether it's going to be a one-handed or two-handed stop.

If you lose sight of the ball for one fleeting moment you are likely to be in trouble. The ball may hit a divot and marginally change course. It may suddenly slow or gain pace.

As you prepare to pounce, be thinking intently. Don't dare to let your thoughts or your gaze stray to the batsmen. But, at the same time, anticipate what they are planning to do. Your task is to gather the ball and return it to the wicketkeeper in the quickest possible time.

It's all very well for fielders to show off and tease the batsmen into going for another suicidal run. If your deliberate hesitation misfires, the joke will be very much on you. And you won't be popular with the rest of the team.

Some fielders snatch at the ball before returning it to the stumper. That shows a lack of composure. I'm no slouch in the field but I always like actually to *feel* the ball in my hand before sending it back.

As a general rule, *use two hands whenever you can*. But sometimes it is a matter of swooping with one hand, maybe with your back momentarily to the wicket. Again don't snatch. Feel that ball. And try to keep yourself balanced.

You may have noticed the way experienced top-class players often adopt safety-first methods, going down on one knee and providing as solid a wall as possible, so that even a bouncing ball can't get past. 'Safety first' should always be in your mind. It's often more important to prevent a second run than aim for a spectacular and optimistic run-out.

If you have a good throwing arm, you'll no doubt find yourself patrolling the boundary at some stage in the game. County cricketers in England, I find, have a tendency to throw high. Personally I advise a lower trajectory. It makes sense – the ball gets there faster.

WICKET
KEEPING

It may come as a surprise to you – but I enjoy taking over the wicketkeeper's gloves. I sometimes jump at the chance in benefit matches. *We should all make a point of learning the skills of other members of the team.*

The stumper has to concentrate as hard as anyone on the field. He's in action for every single ball. No opportunity for him to take a little snooze. If he relaxes his concentration for just one delivery, it'll probably be the moment when the batsman leans out of his crease and a stumping chance might be accepted.

I've always considered the wicketkeeper to be one of the most important members of the side. He can swing the match in the fielding side's favour with just one spectacular leg-side catch. Or he can do quite the opposite if his reflexes are sluggish and he lets four byes slip needlessly away.

During my county and Test career I've talked to many of the finest stumpers in the world – from Australia's exuberant Rodney Marsh to England's own Bob Taylor. They often look especially weary at the end of the day's play. And none has earned that refreshing ritualistic drink more.

The best wicketkeepers aren't the flashiest ones. If you are a stumper, try to make it a rule to do your job as efficiently as possible – with as little fuss and ostentation as possible.

We have all seen the show-offs behind the stumps. They jump around, playing to the gallery. They like everyone to know they are there. They appeal for every half chance, often when the batsman has missed the ball by a mile. And they end up by irritating everyone.

Too much showmanship in sport is misplaced. The greater the flourish, the more likely the ball is to slip through the gloves. Everyone can forgive a trier in cricket. Not too many can forgive an out-and-out show-off.

One former wicketkeeper of fine county standard used to give as his cardinal rule for would-be wicketkeepers: *Keep down as long as you can. And then get up as quickly as possible.*

There's a lot of wisdom in that. Put it into practice and you are halfway there. Just pause and think what is meant by that piece of sound advice. That same ex-wicketkeeper says, 'In your crouching position, you see the ball pitch and try to determine how much it is moving. Then, in effect, you come up with the ball.' It's really a matter of eyelevel. If you're late coming up and the level of the ball is well above you, then you are in trouble.

As I'll never tire of telling schoolboy cricketers, whether they are batsmen or wicketkeepers (maybe both), feel comfortable in whatever you are doing. If you are comfortable, there's a good chance you will also be relaxed. And, of course, balance comes into this.

I like to see wicketkeepers standing at ease, swinging their gloves gently from one side of the body to the other between deliveries. It's like the pendulum of a clock, if you like. It ensures that the player has perfect balance.

Advice can vary on how far apart the feet should be as you crouch. Again, it's a matter of comfort. Always be in a flexed, alert position, poised for the diving catch – or the ball that suddenly turns a yard!

'When do I stand up to the bowler and when back?' It's the inevitable question from the novice keeper. He doesn't want to be accused by his team-mate of being a bit of a coward and retreating unnecessarily for the faster bowlers.

There is often only false courage in standing up to the pace men. Your brief is a simple one. Cut out the extras, and take the catches. If you are obsessed with the idea of courting popularity with your colleagues you could be heading for all sorts of problems. You won't often be in a position to take a catch if you are standing up to the quickies. And the extras will soon be mounting alarmingly.

Jim Parks is perhaps a good example. Technically, he wasn't one of the best wicketkeepers ever to play in county cricket. Yet he was selected for his country because he knew his limitations. He usually stood back – and seldom missed anything.

The West Indies' Jeff Dujon has earned a growing number of admirers, for his batting as well as his wicketkeeping. Here, to my mind, is a player with a thoroughly exciting future

There's ENJOYMENT in the young man's face and that's one of the best starting points of all. He may never be the best wicketkeeper in the school but he'll always do his best – with a smile on his face. 'Learn to swing to your left and right' I tell him. This helps with the balance. The keeper should look relaxed without being careless. He must make sure the ball goes into his gloves and doesn't bounce out again. By agility and hours of practice he can even make a bad return from the outfield look a good one. If he's standing back to the pace bowler, he can 'feel' himself into the ideal position to take the ball at waist height

---

Vision is important. If you are standing back, crouch in the sensible position outside the off stump, so that you can keep your eye on the ball all the way. If you are going for a catch to your right hand – off the right-handed bat, that is – be positive. It will avoid any confusion with first slip. Occasionally you'll get in each other's way. But with practice will come added understanding, and after a time you'll sense which is your catch and which is the one first slip should take.

If you are standing up close, the reflexes have to be that bit sharper. The catch may have to be an instinctive one. You have only a split second, quite often, to whip those bails off as the batsman's heel is momentarily raised. Good luck! But I know what a thrill it is when the square-leg umpire's finger goes up. I see it on the faces of my friends, whether playing for the West Indies or the Rising Sun CC.

So which is the hardest bowler to keep to? Ask any wicketkeeper. The usual answer is, 'The off-spinner.' Even the best stumper will lose sight of the ball as it turns and goes down the leg side. The result is that you go over blind. That is where anticipation and intuition come in.

Don't be put off. It's an exciting position, a key one. The battle of wits between you and the batsman is part of the fun (and the challenge).

Wicketkeeping is, in its way, the number one specialist job in the field. But the stumper mustn't be a loner. He must make it his business to work up an effective relationship during the match with his bowlers. He must get to know their whims and their tricks. He must keep his attention solidly on them from the time they begin their run up.

But you must never assume. Just because your bowling pal has a reputation to seam or swing or spin the ball one particular way, you shouldn't, whatever you do, take it for granted. Whatever the bowler's claims back in the pavilion or during the net sessions about his particular skills, the ball's course is sometimes out of his hands. It may go in the opposite direction. Sometimes the bowler is clever enough to do it on purpose. Ian Botham is usually thought of as an outswinger. But I have seen some excellent inswingers from him.

Nervous young wicketkeepers are apt to snatch the ball. That will never do. Let the ball come to you. That is true whether you are standing back, taking at waist height or up to receive a boundary return.

Just as the team relies on the wicketkeeper, he has every reason to rely on the fielders. The perfect return to him is bail high and straight into his gloves. But, of course, none of us are perfect.

I end this little section with two basic bits of advice. If you play for a village or club side, you'll be coming up against the same opponents each season. Make a mental note of their batsmen's flaws. Maybe one has a tendency to become impatient and to jump down the wicket after a time. Another may be inclined to lift his heel once too often. A third is apt to spar outside the off stump against the medium-paced bowlers.

I know of top-class wicketkeepers who diligently keep a notebook. They retain a record of batsmen's failings – and that makes a lot of sense to me. You don't need to tell anyone. That can be your secret way of totting up the victims.

My second crumb of advice. Study the great players. Televised Test matches provide the ideal opportunity. See how perfectly balanced they are. You won't catch them snatching at the ball. Good luck!

AS I WAS SAYING

ON BEING A CAPTAIN

I wonder whether you are one of those players with leadership qualities. Would you like to end up by captaining your side? Maybe you have already been the skipper in school matches.

Captaincy has nothing at all to do with having the most to say, being the best player in the team or wanting to make every decision on your own. Mind you, it can help if you also happen to be a useful member of the side and have a natural aptitude for working things out in your mind. But captaincy is a lot more than that.

It's a terribly difficult job. You must have noticed how quickly it goes round among our county clubs. Captaining a Test eleven is also no sinecure, as fairly recent cricket history demonstrates. It imposes added strains on the captain and he's usually the poor old fall guy when results go against the team.

I accept that captaining a convivial village and small club side isn't quite the same as leading your country. The village blacksmith isn't going to have all the national sportswriters at his throat if he brings his spin bowlers on too late. But in some respects a captain is a captain – whatever the level of the match.

He must not be above advice. That means he must be prepared to talk to other members of the team. The ultimate responsibility of learning when to declare or how to handle the bowlers must be the captain's. But he must never be so remote or self-important that he cannot go for a second opinion.

He must involve everybody. He must make every member of the side, even the struggling tailenders, feel they have a role to play. He must, by personal example, make sure it's a happy dressing room. Players who bat only for their average must be firmly told that cricket is a team game.

Over a season, a captain is going to make some mistakes – just as every umpire does. But he must be positive, and imaginative. Go for a result if possible. Don't be negative, just for the cussed reason that you want to frustrate the opposition. That is my general advice, although I know that at times a different approach has to be adopted in competitive matches.

The skipper sets the mood. Play with a smile on your face. Encourage a struggling team-mate. Applaud a good catch. Avoid public reprimands; instead, have a discreet private word to a snoozing fielder. And, above all, enjoy your cricket. The rest of the team will follow your lead.

SELF-DISCIPLINE IS IMPORTANT

I've always taken the view that to be a good sportsman you need plenty of self-discipline. And, believe me, I know just how many distractions there can be when you are young.

Maybe there is a strong temptation to miss your club's training night 'just this once' so that you can go to the movies or take your new girlfriend out. I can't stress too strongly the need to train. You'll be surprised how much genuine satisfaction you get from it – and the understanding girlfriend will still be waiting.

We aren't all natural athletes. I used to look with a grin around the Somerset dressing room. We were all shapes and sizes. Out on the field, some moved with far more grace and style than others. Some enjoyed training, a few gritted their teeth (shall we say?) and made the best of it.

I accept that many of you young sportsmen and -women reading this book don't especially like training. My plea to you is to show that bit more determination – it won't be wasted, I promise you. From my days as a teenager I have spent hours, often on my own, trying to make myself a better cricketer. I've done that without a bat and ball.

England's captain David Gower at his most fluent

There are many advantages in having someone to push you. You may be one of the lucky ones who belong to a sports club with a capable and enthusiastic person to coach and encourage you. For one thing, he'll make sure you don't cheat and secretly cut a mile or so off your training run.

Do you know something? I'm feeling fitter these days than when I was actually breaking into cricket. Then I used to depend on my youth and my natural ability. Now I am more conscious of the value of training and fitness. I smile to myself when I hear people whispering that I've had a good life and may be soon over the hill. I don't say anything – but I train that bit harder.

The great fear of professional sportsmen is injury, of course. On one of my visits to Australia I had recurrent back trouble. No one seemed able to diagnose what exactly was the problem or how serious it was. But I got over it, with helpful treatment. Take an intelligent attitude to injuries. If you pull a muscle or take a knock, ask for the right advice – and act on it. The more sensible training you do, the less likely the risk of injury.

KEEP FIT

You've got to work at keeping fit. It's all very well to say that natural ability in a sportsman is enough – I assure you it isn't.

To me, fitness isn't simply a matter of the body. The mind is just as important. You may look in marvellous physical nick. But if the mental attitude isn't right, you might as well stay in the pavilion (or the soccer dressing room). Aim at all times to have your body and mind attuned in perfect harmony.

If you are young and able-bodied, there's really no excuse to become lazy and flabby through lack of exercise. You don't need weights or lots of special equipment. Work out simple routines – a string of exercises – and do them in your own bedroom at the start or the end of the day. Make them a little harder each day.

Jogging has become very popular, of course. That's one good idea – and there is positively no age barrier. Frankly, I've never really liked road work. It doesn't seem to suit me. Swimming is different. That to me is the ideal way of getting fit. It seems to involve every muscle in the body. Home in Antigua,

I wander off to one of our lovely beaches, three or four miles long. Keeping fit in the water is never a lonely occupation for me. I know it's doing me good.

As a cricketer, I need to keep my back strong and free from strains. I concentrate a great deal on my abdominal muscles, and there are many exercises to help them. Watch the players having their physical jerks before a county match. Perhaps you've seen Dennis Waight meting out his 'torture' to the West Indies and the Somerset players. He's a tough Australian who in his time has played Rugby League and been an amateur boxer of some repute. You don't argue with a guy like that!

You can learn from people like Dennis how to keep fit and tone up the muscles. A few joints will creak to begin with and you may feel a little stiff next morning. But you'll sense that you are in better shape. There's nothing wrong in taking a pride in your physical condition (that's nothing at all to do with vanity, more with common sense). Maybe you'll never be a very talented sportsman. My words are intended for you, just as much as for the stars of the school XI. Fitness is terribly important.

But I end with a warning. Do pace yourselves. Don't overdo it. Don't turn fitness into an obsessive fetish. I've suffered from overtraining, ending up exhausted and with sore tummy muscles. That's self-defeating. That makes no sense at all. Keep it in perspective – and at all times *enjoy* it.

THERE'S NO FUTURE IN ARGUING

Well, yes, there was that match I played for Antigua against St Kitt's rather a long time ago. I hoped you wouldn't mention that. I'm not particularly proud of what happened – though there was so much conflicting advice being offered me and I didn't know whether I was coming or going!

That was the occasion when I was given out – and I didn't walk. Six thousand spectators worked themselves up into quite a state. Most of them seemed to think the umpire had boobed. There were demonstrations and hastily improvised placards were produced with the ultimatum: No Vivi, No Play. Looking back, it's all somewhat embarrassing. My behaviour that day was out of character. Too many people were trying to manipulate me in the incidents that followed. For my pains, I was suspended for two years.

I have, of course, matured since then. That extraordinary scene was such a lesson to me. It taught me the folly of dissent, even though I felt I had strong grounds for disputing an official's decision.

There's far too much dissent in professional sport these days. You see it on television, among footballers. You see it on tennis courts (and how!). And, I'm sorry to say, you occasionally see it in first-class cricket.

When a player comes up to me after he's been given out to a dubious LBW decision, I give him a word or two of consolation and then a slow grin. Then I'm apt to say, 'Try to forget it. In cricket as in life, we win some and we lose some. In the end there's some kind of balance.'

I'm horrified when I hear of schoolboys showing dissent in sport. I have a terrible feeling that they are often aping what they see on the telly. In this respect, professional sportsmen have a great responsibility.

This is the basic point. Dissent is pointless. However much you argue, you can't reverse the umpire's decision. So you are wasting time and energy – and earning yourself a bad reputation in the process.

By the law of averages, we're all going to get some bad decisions given against us. Umpires are human too. But cheer up – a few borderline decisions are likely to go in our favour.

As batsmen we hate being given out. Yet how often are we the best judge of whether the ball would have gone on to hit the wicket, for instance?

DON'T LET THEM RATTLE YOU

Perhaps I ought to have a word or two about intimidation. And I'm not just thinking about past experiences of mine out in Australia against, for instance, Messrs Lillee and Pascoe. It happens in a great many club matches too, I'm sorry to say.

Now it's all very well of me to say blithely that you should ignore the verbal threats and all the other murmurings that are directed from some bowlers – or, at times, close fielders – to new batsmen. It's gamesmanship, a ploy to undermine your confidence.

Almost as bad is the wicketkeeper who allows everyone for miles hear his gasp, implying that the ball missed your stumps by a coat of paint. It was

Left foot well down – and an on-driven boundary

probably nothing of the sort. We've all heard those infuriating stumpers who repeatedly shout to the bowler, 'Great ball . . . had him beaten all the way. You'll get him next time.'

Well, grit your teeth and make jolly good care that he doesn't. Use it to motivate you. That's what I do. Whenever the Aussies are at their noisiest – and a few of their bowlers at their most frequent with the threats – I say to myself, 'I'll knock that arrogance out of you. You aren't going to frighten me.'

Treat them as bullies. Do your best to ignore their pathetic claims but, whatever you do, don't become complacent in the process.

They are intent in 'talking you out'. Your intent must be to show you are good and completely unruffled at your trade. Once you have made your point, they'll usually give up that particular form of mental warfare and revert to the more acceptable challenge of bat against ball.

'Listen,' I tell boys when they occasionally come up to me and say they hear a specific bowler does his best to talk a batsman out as soon as he gets to the crease, 'that noisy so-and-so has got two arms and two legs. That's exactly what you've got. Go out and prove you're the equal of him.'

A MATTER OF TEMPERAMENT

It's terribly important to keep your emotions under control. Opponents will sometimes work very hard and cleverly to try to fluster you or provoke a reaction. This kind of thing goes on at all levels, I'm afraid. It's known as gamesmanship, as I've already said.

Perhaps you have just reached the wicket when you hear a conversation going on implying what a good bowler you are about to face! It's all meant to affect your concentration and undermine your confidence. Don't let it.

And then there are the spectators. If you are playing in a club match there may only be half a dozen people watching. But they may be supporting the other side and won't let you forget it. Barracking is part of the game and we have to accept it. Much of it is good-natured, anyway. That is always guaranteed to add to the spirit of the game.

What about it when occasionally the remarks carry a sting and turn to insults? I know all about that. There have been some very tactless and unkind things shouted at me. One or two Yorkshire crowds will know what I'm referring to. I've tried to develop the most effective technique for dealing with my insensitive critics. I grip my bat that bit tighter and will myself to provide the best answer of all – by reaching three figures. That gives me the greatest satisfaction and it channels any temporary anger in the right direction.

But we're only human. Some of my friends claim that I have at times a shortish fuse. I can only say that I try my hardest to shut cruel remarks from my mind. My advice to young sportsmen who are honest enough to admit that they have a slight problem over temperament is to make sure that their feelings are kept out of sight. Once you are rattled, your play is bound to suffer. And that's a moral victory for the opposition.

We could all name a few bad sportsmen. They are never out. They never get LBW decisions that their bowling deserves. They are always victims of bad declarations. In short, there is invariably something wrong. That is no way to *enjoy* your cricket. I assure you I love my cricket, whether I've been playing for Rising Sun (home in Antigua), Lansdown, Somerset or the West Indies. Friends tell me it shows in my demeanour. Cricket is a *happy* game – as well as a great one. I discovered that long ago.

Collective Caribbean joy. Malcolm Marshall traps Pringle LBW in the 1984 Test at Headingley. I see nothing wrong in expressing our delight as a team. Of course, we're an exuberant nation!

DRESSING ROOM DANGERS

As a batsman, it's essential to be composed while you are at the wicket. But remember that it's equally important to be composed and capable of making your own judgements *before* you reach the square.

You will know, I'm sure, what I mean. There is too often the temptation to be influenced by what others are saying. Don't allow your confidence to be drained away by senseless gossip and fears expressed in the dressing rooms. It is something I feel very strongly about.

We've all heard it. There we are strapping on our pads, being forced to listen to the running commentary of team mates who seem intent on self-destruction. 'Did you see that?' 'He's the fastest we've come up against this season.' 'He can really dig 'em in.' 'Dangerous, that's what he is.'

That psychology is a disaster. Such alarmist comments are liable to ruin the confidence of susceptible young players. They breed unnecessary agitation and plant added anxieties in everyone's mind. Whenever I hear a colleague giving us a terrifying rundown of what is in store, I feel like retorting, 'For heaven's sake, shut up!' It does no good at all.

There is only one person to make a judgement – and that is yourself. As a batsman, once you get to the wicket the game is a personal challenge between you and the bowler. You must treat every ball intelligently *on its merit*. That has nothing to do with what has gone on ten minutes before, relayed to you by an apprehensive team-mate.

Be sensibly wary by all means. If you know the particular bowler can swing the ball away and the conditions are humid, then be that extra bit cautious. But never, never, never be overawed by reputation. Go to the wicket the equal (mentally) of the bowler. Whatever his known ability, whether he's an exciting county prospect or plays in the neighbouring village or rival school side, he will be human enough to make errors. If you listen to all the nonsense in advance, you will end up treating him with too much respect. That will never do!

In character and personality, we are all different. Some like to sit alone before it's their turn to bat. Others remain as gregarious as ever. Do whatever is right for you. I like to sit with others, sharing in the normal dressing room chats and jokes.

Mind you, it isn't just the batsmen who are apt to get in a bit of a state about what they are going to meet out in the middle. What I have just been saying applies just as much to bowlers. Don't be overawed by a batsman's reputation.

RUNNING BETWEEN THE WICKET

Are you one of those unlucky batsmen who is always getting run-out? Or worse, are you the chap with a reputation for running out your teammates?

Some of us are better – or less successful – than others. The stumps are only 22 yards apart and it should, in theory, be the easiest thing in the world to chase from one end to the other. In fact, it can be perilously difficult.

We can all name established county players who have always been bad judges of a run. It's the same in your local team, I have no doubt. But, honestly, it needn't be. Learn from your mistakes.

Don't try to be too clever. You've seen top-class cricketers appearing not to need to call at all because of the rapport that they've built up. That isn't often the case of all. It's just that with the understanding they have built up over the years, they can make their intentions clear with the minimum of noise.

My advise to you is to call – LOUD AND CLEAR. Even when a couple of runs are obsolutely certain, you should still tell your partner what you want. And let there be no confusion at all about who is calling. You know the rule – in front of the wicket it's the striker's call, behind it's up to the non striker. That's really only common sense.

In almost every match, whatever the standard, we see at least one example of terrible running between the wickets. I hope I don't sound smug when I say there is really no excuse. *Be confident and positive . . . and get cracking.*

So often singles are there for the taking. They may be sharp – but they aren't suicidal. If you make a quick judgment – and your partner is alert and eager – you'll be surprised how much quicker the scoreboard moves along. Bowlers and fielding sides don't like you to snap up these quick runs. It makes them edgy – and perhaps erratic. They will be inclined to misfield the ball more frequently.

And that brings me to a gentle warning. It's one of the oldest in the game, of course. Don't automatically treat a piece of misfielding as a run-bonus. Be extra wary about setting off, and be extra sure the fielder isn't going to recover and shy in before you can make your ground. Honestly, I've lost count of the number of times batsmen have got themselves out, trying to take advantage of a moment of apparently sloppy fielding.

It's a wise rule to go like the clappers for the first run. And be as nimble and crisp as you can on the turn, if you are coming for a second.

Finally, *don't be selfish*. There are *two* batsmen at the wicket and survival is equally important to both of them. Just don't let me see you putting your partner in peril!

THE VALUE OF ENCOURAGEMENT

Cricket is a team game. The dressing room is a small community. We are friends with equal interests, able to share our confidences. Some players may be better than others. Some, those in the first-class game, have a more glamorous life than others. But we are at the same time a close-knit family.

It's an odd fact that I'm more of an outgoing person among other cricketers in the dressing room. I warm to the camaraderie, the in jokes, the chatter.

For a county cricketer, there is a good deal of travelling involved. That can lead to fatigue and boredom. It's essential that we lift each other's spirits and enjoy each other's company. A sense of humour is vital. My pal Ian Botham is quite a practical joker.

I have always tried to make it my business to encourage younger players. If they carry off a fine catch, I run over to pat them on the back. Some fuddy-duddies don't apparently approve of such public shows of delight. I see nothing wrong with them. If one of the young guys in the team does something especially well, I want him to know that we appreciate it. I think it's true to say I'm one of the first, quite often, to extend my congratulations. I remember from my young days what that kind of fillip meant.

My plea to older players in club cricket is never to forget the importance of encouragement. It's all too easy for the more experienced cricketers to get rather cynical – and to be perhaps unnecessarily mean with their compliments.

When I first got into the West Indies side and was going through a shaky

patch, I remember how Clive Lloyd and one or two of the others came across to me in the dressing room, where I was slumped dejectedly on a bench, and offered some consolation. They encouraged me to start smiling again.

Well, it worked in my case. We won the next match by an innings at Delhi and I scored 192 not out. I honestly believe that if I'd failed again, at that tender stage of my Test career, my world would have collapsed. Thanks, lads, for that lift back in 1974. There really is a moral to be gained from my experience.

RATION THE HEROICS

Cricket writers were always inclined to note the fact that I batted without a helmet. I also admitted in the first of my autobiographies that throughout my early career as a school and club player I seldom bothered about wearing a box. They were statements of fact – and I wasn't particularly proud of them.

My advice to any young cricketer is this. Protect yourself. Don't try to be a hero. First-class players supposedly walk to the wicket these days in a sheet of armour! That is their choice – and they should certainly not be criticized for ensuring that their livelihood is not put in jeopardy.

It's partly true that for a long time I resisted the helmet because it kept me that bit sharper and added to the competitive edge in my game. I was facing up to the challenge of the fast bowler and not allowing him any psychological advantage. But I had the good fortune to be able to pick the ball up very quickly. I had the God-given gift of perfect eyesight.

Now I'm getting older and I accept that I'm no longer picking up that little cherry quite so soon. You will be seeing me more and more in a helmet.

In club matches there may not be as many fearsome bowlers around. At the same time, I seriously advise you to take what protection is necessary. That is also true when you go into the nets. It's all very well to think you are just having a gentle warm-up. The ball can fly about quite alarmingly on some of the rough strips that are used for net practice. There's nothing worse than getting injured in the nets – at least it seems worthwhile if you are out in the middle.

A moment of contemplation

Thigh guards and, of course, a box are often obligatory. I don't personally go in for arm protection. It restricts my freedom of movement. But I would leave that decision to the individual – and the strength and pace of the opposing attack!

On the subject of what to wear, I'd like to throw in a timely word about sweaters. *Do keep warm.* Cricket can be very cold in England during the early part of the season. Your muscles and overall coordination will let you down if you are shivering. Again, wear what is right and comfortable for you. You won't often see me, in England, batting in a long-sleeve sweater. I like my arms to be as free and loose as possible. Against that, I know some club cricketers who tell me they feel they have added protection (at least in the mind) if they have thick sweaters down to the wrists.

THE DANGERS OF OVERCONFIDENCE

It's been suggested to me at times that I never suffer from butterflies in the tummy before I go in to bat. Don't you believe it. I've had my share of Test cricket around the world, but I still get nervous on occasions. And that isn't at all a bad thing.

Let me try to explain. It's very important to be relatively relaxed and in control as you walk to the wicket. If you are a bundle of nerves, then you are more likely to give your wicket away. But, at the same time, there are advantages in being quite tense.

I've never been on the stage, but all the best actors are supposed to get very nervous as they wait in the wings, irrespective of the amount of experience they have. It's said that they can then channel this nervous energy into their performance. This also applies up to a point in cricket.

This is the moment when I confess that I have been overconfident at times. I've picked up my bat and strolled out to the square with all the relaxation in the world. And it has occasionally let me down. I can remember a few innings of mine which came to an abrupt conclusion because I was overconfident. Do try to learn from that past mistake of mine.

Relaxation is a marvellous ability. It gives you the mental strength to take on the best bowlers – and believe that you can get the ball away to the boundary. But, *please*, never allow a healthy amount of relaxation to turn into a fatal cockiness. It'll be your undoing. You'll leave yourself open and start taking too many risks too early.

From time to time in this book I have reminded you of the importance of the right mental attitude. Let me be personal again. Perhaps I've had a slightly hectic time the night before. Perhaps I have a private problem or two on my mind. As a cricketer, I must steel myself to shut such matters out of my thoughts. It seems a slightly harsh thing, but there must be no preoccupations or distractions once the sportsman is out on the field.

Returning to my earlier theme, confidence is one thing. It's an essential ingredient for any sportsman – whether he's knocking over stumps, kicking goals or scoring tries. Overconfidence is quite another. You'd better do something about it. If you are too conceited to accept it, then I hope your best friend will tell you. And quickly.

WE ALL HAVE BAD SPELLS

Cricket can become very depressing when the runs or the wickets aren't coming. Players find it hard to hide their emotions. They mope around in private agony. I've seen them doing it in the Somerset and even the West Indies teams. There are few other games in which a player can become so dispirited through lack of form. A footballer can make a mistake and it's forgotten in the course of the other 89 minutes. In cricket, the poor batsman makes a single mistake – and he's usually straight back to the pavilion.

In some ways there's something unfair about cricket. If a player is struggling for form, he always seems to be given a brute of a ball right at the start of his innings. Or maybe he's on the receiving end of a bad LBW decision.

I'd be dishonest if I said that I never got depressed as a player. Of course I do – after a lapse of concentration and maybe a simple catch to mid-wicket. At the same time, I'm cross with myself for letting the team down. But I have always made a very conscious effort to offset any hint of being down in the dumps. I know I must put on a brave face and have a pint after the day's play just as normal, as though I'm in top nick. That is important for my own state of mind. Depression compounds lack of confidence. And it becomes a vicious circle.

I've always taken the view that cricket is a great leveller. I know in my heart that I'm capable of playing very well indeed – and also of playing very badly. We must all be honest enough to admit this. The good and the bad even themselves out. That disappointing run won't go on for ever. Soon you'll be back with the strokes.

It's the same with bowlers. You may suddenly feel you have lost your touch completely. If you are a spinner, maybe the knack appears to have deserted you for a few weeks. Don't panic. Get to work in the nets. Take helpful advice. Tell yourself you'll very soon be back among the wickets again.

Let's get serious for a moment. It's all part of life. Up and down. No one can expect to be a success all the time. And, after all, isn't it a bit selfish to think it's got to be you who goes out and dominates play? There are ten other players in your side. Why shouldn't they sometimes succeed, rather than you?

All the great sportsmen in history – whether Sir Jack Hobbs, Bobby Charlton or Cliff Morgan – have had lean spells. They knew that they would fight their way out of them. Some players try too hard. That works against them and they continue to struggle.

WE CAN INVENT TOO MUCH

Cricket has become a great deal more competitive – even at the most modest local level. Village teams, who used only to play leisurely friendly matches on Saturday afternoons, now belong to leagues. And they are intent on *winning*.

There is absolutely nothing wrong with that. If we didn't want to win, cricket would have hardly any point at all. With increased competitive enthusiasm have come a number of bonuses. The standard of fielding has improved out of all recognition. That is true at all levels – county and parish.

I hope the schoolboys reading this book will also play to win. That shouldn't be confused with a lessening sportsmanship or losing enjoyment, although I'm sorry to say that occasionally that tendency creeps in. Don't ever be guilty of taking your cricket so seriously that the fun is sacrificed. That is a passionate plea of mine.

But there are a few other dangers that come with limited-over cricket. I'll mention just one. We call it improvisation – or making unnatural strokes to keep up with the clock.

Maybe you think it's a little odd for me to sound a warning about improvisation! After all, I have been known to take a few liberties in an effort to adjust the run rate. My efforts to wrest the initiative back and, at the same time, knock the bowlers off their length may find favour with the crowd. But I privately get less pleasure from the kind of shot that I know wouldn't please my old sports masters back in St John's.

County cricketers are having to revise their techniques all the time, coming to terms with 40 overs on Sundays, 60 overs or three-day county matches, not to mention five-day Tests. It's a disconcerting mixture. One-day matches, whatever their exciting appeal, have spoilt pure cricket up to a point.

We have to invent shots. To me the one-day match is a 'number job'. I love playing in them and accept how as contests they are ideal for the spectators as they bring a result the same day. But inventions in cricket are fraught with pitfalls.

County players, turning to the John Player competition, can't wait around for the bad ball. They have to treat nearly every good ball as a bad one. There's no question of playing deliveries on merit.

If you are a natural attacking batsman, the last thing I want to do is dissuade you from going for your shots. I approve of aggressive batting. But all I ask is that you don't forget everything you were ever taught in the mad pursuit of the 'numbers job'. Batting really is an art form. Don't devalue it.

GAINING INSIGHTS

I rather enjoy my bit of bowling, whether off breaks or my gentle seamers. But it isn't ever likely to go to my head. I don't look on myself as an all-rounder.

One of the reasons why I enjoy bowling is that it gives me added insights into batting. The opportunities I have had as a modest bowler have turned me into a better batsman.

That probably calls for some explanation. The bowler has a special vantage point in relation to the batsman. He, better than anyone, can observe what is

FOURPENNETH!

going through the batsman's mind. And he can study at close hand the finesse – and the flaws – of the man he is facing.

It also works the other way round, of course. The batsman, with an alert, open mind, can learn a great deal about bowling techniques. It's all part of the vital process of concentration. Make yourself tick over mentally all the time. If you're batting, appreciate a good delivery – and learn from it. If you're bowling, privately appreciate the perfectly timed stroke, even if it is at your expense!

As a batsman, I have always looked on bowling a few overs as valuable therapy. It keeps me involved in the game. If I also have the good luck to take a wicket, my spirits soar.

This brings me to the subject of *involvement*. My emphatic advice to you all is to will yourself to be in the action as much as possible. As a fielder, I want the ball to come in my direction every time. I want every catch to come to me. If the ball is running towards the boundary, I want to be the chap sprinting after it.

We spend a lot of time in the field. And we aren't all going to be given an over or two. So it's important to enjoy our fielding. Don't get bored – it will show on your face. Keep on your toes and be hungry for a catch. Tactics are a big part of the challenge. You may not be the skipper but there's nothing to stop you pitting your skills, privately and tactically, against the opposition. Anything to maintain your involvement.

One last word. There is nothing worse than the sight of a fielder who seems to have lost interest in the match. When Brian Close first came to Somerset he decided that one or two players had a tendency to doze off in the field. He soon put a stop to that. However good you are and whatever the club you play for – maybe it's the village 3rd XI – involve yourself in every ball. I can recommend it.

AT LEAST LOOK THE PART

I've always been clothes-conscious. I like to look smart, whether I'm out on the field or with friends during the evening. This has nothing to do with conceit.

When I walk out with the team I'm proud of my appearance. My flannels are freshly laundered and creased. My cricket boots have been cleaned. I'm being paid to play cricket – and I want to look the part. I owe that to the supporters.

No one will ever accuse me of being a scruffy cricketer. Self-pride and self-confidence are closely linked. I hate to see a player shuffle onto the field in dirty flannels, which still show the signs of where he polished the ball the previous day.

It doesn't matter whether you're playing for your school team or on the village green. Try to look smart. I believe appearance gives one a lift.

They used to say that when Wally Hammond walked out to bat for Gloucestershire and England, he had the appearance of a prince. And that was what they dubbed him. My friends all tell me that Sir Frank Worrell was also a splendid sight as he strode to the wicket.

Off the field, styles have changed, of course. You can wear a T-shirt and still look decent. You no longer need to wear a collar and tie to be presentable. The most important thing is to be clean and tidy.

These stray thoughts may seem odd coming from me in a book aimed primarily for young and potential cricketers. But to have a neat, dignified, self-confident appearance is part of my philosophy.

I can assure you of one thing. If you're a slovenly individual in the street, the chances are that those same qualities will be reflected in your approach to the game.

THERE'S MORE TO LIFE THAN CRICKET

For more than ten years now I've played cricket summer and winter. There hasn't been much let-up. 'Don't you get fed up with it, Viv?', people ask. Why should I? I have been blessed with a natural talent to hit a cricket ball. The game has given me so much enjoyment – and I hope it shows.

But I do get rather jaded at times. Some of my friends at Taunton claim that I occasionally look weary when I report for pre-season training at Somerset. I have probably just got back from a demanding tour.

That all-the-year-round schedule doesn't apply to club players, of course. All the same, I always tell them never to get the game out of perspective. As I grow older and no doubt more mature, I increasingly realize that there is more to life than cricket.

You'll forgive me for being serious just for a moment, but I'm trying to make a point. Perhaps you have three ducks in a row and your world is collapsing. Maybe you just can't take a wicket – and you are carrying your disappointments home with you to depress the rest of the family. That is a selfish thing to do.

A large proportion of my earnings come from cricket and it is my career. At the same time, I work hard to make myself a broader person. I love sailing. I play a bit of tennis and golf. On the odd occasion I'm in England during the

Family times at our Taunton home. With my wife Miriam and our two children

winter, I make an effort to see my favourite football team, Liverpool. My first visit to Anfield was one of the greatest thrills of my life. I love my reggae music. I love family life. My idea of a perfect evening is to get together with my friends – and talk. Just so long as it isn't small talk.

I can't emphasize too strongly how important fellowship is. Back in Antigua, I discovered that it was almost as much fun sharing a can of beer in the clubhouse or the local bar after a match as it was being out on the square.

I'm a bit of an idealist. And I honestly believe the genuine friendships made *after* a match are as important, and certainly more long-standing, than the result.